PEOPLE WHO MADE A DIFFERENCE

MAHATMA GANDHI

D0170716

Other titles in the
PEOPLE WHO MADE A DIFFERENCE
series include

Marie Curie
Father Damien
Bob Geldof
Martin Luther King, Jr.
Mother Teresa

North American edition first published in 1990 by
Gareth Stevens Children's Books
1555 North RiverCenter Drive, Suite 201
Milwaukee, Wisconsin 53212, USA

First published in the United Kingdom in 1989. This edition
is abridged from the original published in 1987 by Exley
Publications Ltd. and written by Michael Nicholson.
Copyright © 1987 by Exley Publications. Additional end
matter © 1990 by Gareth Stevens, Inc.

Library of Congress Cataloging-in-Publication Data

Birch, Beverley.
    Mahatma Gandhi : champion of human rights / by Michael
Nicholson ; this edition written by Beverley Birch. — North
American ed.
        p.   cm. — (People who made a difference)
    Summary: Follows the life of the statesman who was a key
figure in India's fight for independence from Great Britain.
        ISBN 0-8368-0390-6
        1. Gandhi, Mahatma, 1869-1948—Juvenile literature.
    2. Nationalists—India—Biography—Juvenile literature.
    3. Statesmen—India—Biography—Juvenile literature. [1. Gandhi,
    Mahatma, 1869-1948. 2. Statesmen.] I. Nicholson, Michael, 1937-
    Mahatma Gandhi. II. Title. III. Series.
    DS481.G3B483   1990   954.03'5'092—dc20
    [B]   [92]   89-77589

**For a free color catalog describing
Gareth Stevens' list of high-quality
children's books, call**

**1-800-341-3569 (USA) or
1-800-461-9120 (Canada)**

BBC Hulton Picture Library — 31, 42;
Camera Press —12, 26, 58, 59; Tom
Hanley — 24, 25, 44, 52, 61; Indo-British
Films Ltd. — 20-21, 28-29, 32, 36-37, 40,
53, 57; the MacQuitty International
Photographic Collection — 6 (top);
National Army Museum — 15 (both),
30; National Gandhi Museum, New
Delhi — 11, 13, 16, 19, 38 (below), 54, 56;
Ann and Bury Peerless Slide Resources
and Picture Library — 6 (below); the
Photo Source — 4, 17, 43, 50, 55; Paul
Popper Ltd. — 38 (top), 48, 51; Tom
Redman — cover illustration; the Royal
Commonwealth Society — 9 (both), 10;
BK Sinha — 49.
    The map on page 62 is reproduced
by kind permission of the Press Infor-
mation Bureau, Government of India.

Our grateful thanks go to Sir Richard
Attenborough and Indo-British Films
Ltd. for permission to reproduce stills
from the film *Gandhi*.

Series conceived and edited by Helen Exley
Series editors, U.S.: Amy Bauman and Rhoda Irene Sherwood
Additional end matter, U.S.: Meredith Ackley
Research editor, U.S.: John D. Rateliff
Cover design: Kate Kriege

Printed in Hungary

1 2 3 4 5 6 7 8 9 9 96 95 94 93 92 91 90

PEOPLE
WHO MADE
A DIFFERENCE

Champion of human rights

MAHATMA GANDHI

Beverley Birch's adaptation of the book by Michael Nicholson

Gareth Stevens Children's Books
MILWAUKEE

The beginning

No one likes to feel unwanted or to be insulted. When, as a young lawyer, Mohandas Gandhi moved to South Africa, he learned that Indian people were often disliked and insulted. Barbers refused to cut his hair. He could not stay in hotels where white people stayed. A stagecoach driver beat him when he refused to give his seat to a white passenger. Gandhi was put off a train by a policeman because a white passenger refused to share a compartment with a brown-skinned Indian. He spent the night in a station waiting room.

That night, Gandhi thought about his future in that country. He had three choices. He could ignore the insults and carry on as though they weren't happening. He could go back home to India. Or he could stay and fight it. Gandhi decided it was his duty to stay and use his knowledge of law to fight for the nonwhite people of South Africa.

Gandhi described this as a turning point in his life. At twenty-four years

"It has always been a mystery to me how men can feel themselves honoured by the humiliation of their fellow beings."

Mahatma Gandhi,
in South Africa

5

Above: Gandhi's tomb, with the Hindi words "Hey Rama." In English, this means "Oh God." These were Gandhi's last words as he died.

Right: Gandhi's statue outside the house in Porbandar, India, where he was born. There are statues and memorials to him all over India. Most Indians think of him as their greatest leader and saint.

old, he was a shy, young Indian lawyer. But he became a passionate fighter for human freedom. For the next fifty years, he fought against the things he thought were wrong and unfair. He fought not with weapons but with words and ideas, by example and by self-sacrifice.

In South Africa, and later in India, Gandhi taught his followers to face the British guns and sticks with organized, unarmed protest. When these protesters, which included thousands of women, were attacked and beaten, they did not strike back. Gandhi taught his followers this way of disobeying unfair laws and rules. It is called *satyagraha*. He showed them how to protest in an organized, completely nonviolent way. The people were prepared to break laws that they thought were wrong, and go to jail — by the thousands.

His teachings spread from South Africa to India. Eventually they were known all over the world. His methods give people who have no freedom or justice a way to fight without having to kill. By the time he died, this gentle, smiling man was honored by hundreds of millions of Indians and by people throughout the world. The United Nations in New York stopped discussions when news of his death reached them. They knew the world had lost one of its strongest voices for peace.

"Mahatma Gandhi will go down in history on a par with Buddha and Jesus Christ."
Viscount Louis Mountbatten,
the last British viceroy
of India

"To observe at first hand ... the towering greatness, the goodness, the high spirits and humor, the humility ... the genius, of this man was the greatest stroke of fortune that ever befell me."
William L. Shirer,
Pulitzer Prize-winning
author of The Rise and Fall
of the Third Reich

Child of India

Mohandas Karamchand Gandhi was born at Porbandar, India, on October 2, 1869. At that time, India was ruled by Britain. Already, more than 200 million people lived in India. This was seven times as many people as Britain and Ireland had.

India was a land of contrasts: desert plains, vast rivers, swamps, thick jungles, and the highest mountains on earth. India's great size meant that its people were separated from each other. It was difficult getting from one region to another. There were also different religions, habits, and over three hundred languages. Even people of the same religion did not always follow the same beliefs and customs.

The British had been in India since the early seventeenth century when they set up trading posts by force, bribery, or arrangement with the Mogul emperor and the local princes. India was a land of great poverty and vast riches. The rich few did nothing for themselves. There was always a servant close by to wash them, pour them a drink, or fan them if it was hot.

There were many different religions in India. Most people were Hindus. The Muslims made up the second largest group. Communities of Buddhists, Christians, and Jews formed other large

Opposite: Gandhi grew up in the India of the British Empire.

Top: The British king, George V, fires at a tiger in the grass in 1911. His total kill was twenty-four. His party killed thirty-nine tigers, eighteen rhinoceroses, and four bears.

Bottom: The other kind of India that Gandhi saw as a young man: the mace bearers dressed in scarlet and gold at a Delhi durbar *ceremony under British rule.*

Many Europeans had Indian servants who saw to all their needs. The pay was less than half the pay for a similar job in England. This photograph from 1850 shows a man being shaved by his servant.

groups. The Parsees, who had originally come from Persia, worshipped fire as a symbol of God. Primitive tribal groups lived in the hills and forests.

Each group had different beliefs and customs. The cow was sacred to devout Hindus. Most of them were vegetarians — they ate no meat. Muslims ate beef but believed that pork was unclean.

In 1869, the year of Gandhi's birth, Britain's grip on India tightened. The Suez Canal opened that year. This canal connected the Mediterranean Sea with the Indian Ocean by way of the Red Sea. British ships no longer had to sail all the way around Africa to reach India. So the links of trade between the two countries grew stronger. But by the time Gandhi died, seventy-nine years later, Britain no longer controlled India. Gentle Gandhi played a great part in this change.

Boy bridegroom

Mohandas Gandhi was a Hindu, born into the Vaisya *caste*. This was the third of four castes, or groups, in Hindu society. It was below the castes of the respected Brahmins (priests) and the Kshatriyas (soldiers or rulers). But it was above the Sudra (worker) caste. Below all the castes were the people who had no caste. These people were known as the Untouchables or "outcasts." These were the people who carried out the most

Gandhi at seven. He was very close to his mother, Putali Ba. She was very religious. Gandhi lived his whole life according to what she taught him.

unpleasant, dirty tasks in Hindu society — like cleaning the bathrooms. They were thought to be so low that other Hindus believed they would be made dirty if even their shadows were touched by Untouchables. The Untouchables were the people Gandhi later called the Harijans, meaning "Children of God."

Gandhi's father, Karamchand, was an official at the prince of Porbandar's court and became the small state's first minister. Putali Ba, his mother, was very religious. She prayed at each meal and often went completely without food.

Mohandas Gandhi (right) and his older brother, photographed when Gandhi was fourteen. Gandhi was the fourth and last child in his family.

This is called fasting. She also visited the Hindu temple often and did not care for luxuries. His mother's beliefs influenced Gandhi deeply from a very early age.

Gandhi and his family were strict vegetarians. A Muslim friend once tempted Gandhi to eat goat meat. The boy told Gandhi that eating goat would make him strong enough to push the British out of India. Gandhi ate the meat. But all it did was give him terrible nightmares. He was very sorry that he had done it.

When he was thirteen years old, Gandhi was married to Kasturba, the daughter of a Porbandar merchant. It was the custom then, and still is in parts of India, that parents choose someone for their child to marry. The bride and groom do not meet until the wedding.

Student days

In 1888, Gandhi set out on a three-week voyage to London, where he was to study law. He was only nineteen, but he was already a father. His first son, Harilal, had been born some months earlier.

Gandhi vowed that while he was in London, he would not touch wine, women, or meat. His beliefs cut him off from many of his fellow students. He was lonely for his family and his home. He wrote, "I would continually think of my home and country. . . . Everything was strange . . . the people, their ways, and even their dwellings."

Yet Gandhi wanted to fit in as much as possible. For a time, he tried to dress as the other students dressed. One student recalled meeting Gandhi in London in 1890. Gandhi was "wearing a high silk top hat burnished bright, a stiff and starched white collar, and a rather flashy tie that displayed all the shades of the rainbow, under which there was a fine striped silk shirt . . . a morning coat, a double-breasted waistcoat and dark

As a young man, Gandhi dressed in European clothes. During his time in London, he did not wear Indian dress. More than ten years later, he again began to wear Indian-style clothes. Then he dressed as a holy man in simple peasant clothes.

Opposite, top: British soldiers of the Royal Inniskilling Fusiliers in South Africa during the Boer War (1899-1902). Gandhi was given two war medals for forming and leading the Indian Ambulance Corps.

striped trousers to match. . . ." He also carried leather gloves and a silver-mounted stick." This is very different from the Gandhi, dressed in a *dhoti* (a white homespun loincloth), sandals, and a shawl, that the world came to know.

After two years and eight months in England, Gandhi passed his final examinations at the Inner Temple Inn of Court in London. By June 1891, he was qualified to begin work as a lawyer. He was twenty-two years old and had completed studies in French, Latin, physics, and common and Roman law.

But Gandhi did not yet seem to be the man who would inspire millions of people. He later called his college days "the time before I began to live."

A new life in South Africa

Returning to India, Gandhi learned that his mother had died. He felt very sad. He had adored her, and he had always shared her strong religious beliefs.

For nearly two years, Gandhi tried to work as a lawyer in Bombay. He had little success. When he stood up in a courtroom, he became so nervous that he was unable to speak. He sat down to the sound of laughter in the courtroom.

Opposite, bottom: Dead soldiers after the Battle of Spion Kop in early 1900. Gandhi's Indian Ambulance Corps went forward to help the wounded under fire, although they were ordered not to by the British general.

Soon, Gandhi was offered the chance to represent a wealthy Indian merchant in South Africa. He left to do one job there but stayed for twenty-one years.

14

SPION'S KOP.
NATAL.
JAN 24TH 1900

15

Gandhi with the Indian Ambulance Corps in the Boer War, 1899. He led a thousand ambulance men. He and his followers believed that the support they gave to the British in the war would make the British treat the Indians better. They were wrong.

At that time, South Africa had more than five black people to every white person. It was a divided society. Even the white people were divided. One group, the Boers, had descended from Dutch settlers. They were fighting the British for control of the country. While Gandhi was in South Africa, the two groups fought a bitter civil war.

The Indian community in South Africa had over 100 thousand people. The Indians had come because they were desperate for work. They did the horrible jobs that the native Africans would not do, such as working on farms and growing sugarcane.

Most of the Indians worked hard but lived in awful poverty in South Africa. But a few made enough money to buy the things that usually only white people could afford. For this, the whites began to hate and fear them. Laws were made taking away the Indians' rights to vote, to own land, and to move around freely.

By 1896, Gandhi was a rich, successful lawyer. He was earning almost $8,000 a year, which is equal to almost $160,000 in today's money. Gandhi was also a leader in the Indian community. As a leader, he urged the Indian people to give up their ideas about caste, which divided one group from another. He urged them to be honest in business so they would be trusted. He taught them to keep clean

Gandhi is surrounded by some of the people he employed in his firm in Johannesburg, South Africa. Gandhi was a successful lawyer and made a lot of money. He was admired by South Africa's Indian community because he was well educated.

and advised them to learn English so that they could talk to others.

Gandhi taught the Indians that if they wanted the rights of British citizens, they must also accept the duties. These duties included supporting Britain in war. So although he was a pacifist — one who believes in peace and is against war — Gandhi urged the Indians to support the British in the Boer War (1899-1902). In that war, Gandhi helped form and train the Indian Ambulance Corps. He led a thousand ambulance men in the war.

But this did not bring the Indians better treatment. In fact, both the provinces of Natal and Transvaal were trying to drive the Indian community from their lands. In December 1902, Gandhi presented the Indians' complaints to the British colonial secretary, Joseph Chamberlain. Transvaal responded with a stream of new rules and regulations for the Indian people. Tension grew between the Indians and the whites.

The first struggles

In 1907, the feelings of injustice in the Indian community came to a boil. A law known as the Black Act demanded that all Indian people must register and have their fingerprints taken. Anyone without a certificate would be imprisoned, fined, or made to leave the country. The Indians knew what the whites planned to do. At an election meeting in January 1907, General Louis Botha said, "If my party is returned to office, we will . . . drive the [Indians] out of the country within four years."

At this time, Gandhi first came up with the idea of satyagraha, meaning "holding on to the truth." This is a way of dealing with one's opponents with patience and sympathy to get them to agree to one's demands. Gandhi made strict rules about how followers, or *satyagrahis*, should behave. They must not fight back when insulted, beaten, or

Kasturba, Gandhi's wife, three of his four sons, and a nephew are pictured about 1903. She and Gandhi were close. She stayed with him, supporting him in all he did.

arrested. All must be suffered patiently. The idea was to melt the enemy's heart. After this, whenever the Indians felt they were being treated as second-class citizens, they quietly disobeyed the laws and then accepted their punishment.

In January 1908, Gandhi was arrested when he refused to register under the new laws. He had also urged thousands of other Indians not to register. He was sent to prison for two months. This was to be the first of many times in prison for Gandhi. This time, he served only one month of his sentence.

Many Indians also deliberately broke laws banning Indian immigration by crossing the borders between the

different South African states. Gandhi did so and was jailed twice more. Women joined the struggle in 1913. Their particular complaint was that a judge had ruled that only Christian marriages were legal. All Indian wives then became mistresses and would have no rights. When the illegal border crossings began again, a group of women that Gandhi called the Natal Sisters was arrested.

This scene from the film Gandhi shows Gandhi leading striking miners. When the British soldiers charged them, Gandhi told the men to lie down. He believed that horses could not be forced to trample people. He was right. During his time in South Africa, Gandhi developed many new ways of nonviolent civil disobedience. He would later use these methods in India.

Meanwhile, another group of women from Transvaal made their way into Natal. There, they persuaded Indian miners to lay down their tools and go on strike. Many thousands were sent to prison. As word spread, thousands more workers went on strike.

This time, as Gandhi led his people into the province of Transvaal, he was arrested three times. He was finally imprisoned for three months. Gandhi said, "The real road to . . . happiness lies in going to jail and . . . suffering there [for] one's own country and religion."

By the time Gandhi stopped the satyagraha protest, he was known and respected all over South Africa. Word of his action got to India. The lawyer who was once unable to speak in court had become a famous statesman known for his honesty, skill, and courage.

In June 1914, Gandhi and General Jan Smuts, the white South African leader, came together and worked out an agreement to satisfy the Indian community. Gandhi's method of civil disobedience had been successful. It was the first time any protest like this had ever been successful.

At last, Gandhi felt free to return to India. But before he left, he sent General Smuts a pair of sandals he had made while in prison. Smuts later said, "I have worn these sandals for many a summer since then, even though I may feel that I am not worthy to stand in the shoes of so great a man."

Gandhi's beliefs

During twenty-one years of struggle in South Africa, Gandhi developed deeper religious beliefs. He had always been a Hindu. But now his life centered on the teachings of the Bhagavad Gita, the

"What did Gandhi teach me? I suppose the greatest single thing was to seek the truth, . . . to try to be truthful to oneself as well as to others, . . . to cultivate an inner strength, to be tolerant of others . . . to love, to forgive and not to hate . . . to understand the power of nonviolence."
William L. Shirer, in Gandhi: A Memoir

beautiful Hindu religious work. From this time, his beliefs affected the way he dressed, what he ate, his politics — his whole life.

Gandhi was also influenced by ideas from other religions. He particularly liked Christian hymns and the teachings of Jesus Christ. Christ's Sermon on the Mount, Gandhi said, "went straight to the heart." "Blessed are the meek." "Blessed are the poor, for theirs is the Kingdom of God." "Love your enemies." Jesus' teachings were at the heart of Gandhi's way of life.

Gandhi borrowed ideas freely from other religious groups, too: Buddhists, Jains, Muslims. Partially because of this, some very strict Hindus hated him.

Gandhi believed that one of the greatest Hindu teachings was *samakhava*. This idea teaches that people should not let themselves be upset by pain or pleasure. People should work for what they believe in without fear of failure or hope of success. Gandhi believed that the *way* people did things was as important as what they achieved.

Another principle he followed was *aparigraha*. This principle teaches people to reject money and possessions. People could reach God more easily by being poor and not owning many things.

Ahimsa, or nonviolence to all living things, is another teaching of Hinduism.

"I have not the shadow of a doubt that any man or woman can achieve what I have, if he or she would make the same effort and cultivate the same hope and faith."
Mohandas K. Gandhi

Gandhi's ashram, *or farm, at Sevagram, where spinning is part of daily prayers. All food is grown on the site, and people lead a simple life of poverty. Sevagram Ashram still exists today.*

This means not injuring any living thing. Gandhi would not hurt or eat animals. He would not even kill the deadly snakes that sometimes found their way onto the grounds around his home in South Africa. Instead, he guided them away with sticks.

Gandhi's most famous "weapon" was still satyagraha, the "truth-force." By now, this word had also come to mean nonviolent, or passive, resistance. Gandhi always looked for truth and rejected lies. He taught love of other people and was usually respected, even by people he protested against.

Another of Gandhi's tools was his meditation. By thinking about just one thing for a long time, he was able to totally relax his mind. In this way, he kept himself calm. Even when he was working very hard, sleeping less than four hours a night, he was cheerful, smiling, and joking.

In South Africa, Gandhi tried to train his body and mind. He wanted to learn to control his desire for pleasures of the body. So even though he had become a very successful lawyer, he gave up his wealth, his home, and his fine clothes. He even tried to give away his wife's

A picture from Sevagram Ashram shows Gandhi's bed and belongings at the time of his death in 1948. Gandhi's very simple, very poor way of life made millions of Indians feel he was one of them. They felt he could understand and lead them.

Gandhi and Kasturba soon after they returned to India in 1915. Gandhi now went barefoot. He never again wore Western shoes or clothing.

jewels. Gandhi also asked his family and followers to give up a lot.

Gandhi's time in South Africa changed his life. The nonviolent methods that he taught were based on religious beliefs. His religion would be even more important in India's struggle for freedom. Three-quarters of the Indian people were Hindus. Their religion had survived many wars. For centuries, Muslims had ruled India but had not weakened Hinduism. Gandhi's position as both a religious and political leader would help him lead India in its struggle for freedom from British rule.

Gandhi comes home

Gandhi was forty-five when he returned home to India in 1915. He, Kasturba, and their sons were surprised to be met by huge crowds. Gandhi's work in South Africa had made him famous.

Gandhi decided he must learn more about India's problems. He started an ashram, or farm where many families live and work together. Soon, about two hundred people lived in the community, promising to follow Gandhi's rules. His rules called for them to lead a life of honesty, prayer, and service to others.

Gandhiji* was such a warm person

*The suffix *ji* is added to the end of a name as a sign of affection and respect.

that people wanted to live like him. He soon had many followers. People began calling him *Mahatma*, meaning "great soul." He was known as someone who fought for people's rights. He supported the Untouchables, the peasants, and the factory workers. He aided the mill workers of Ahmedabad in a strike against their employers and the farmers of Gujarat in a fight against unjust taxes.

During World War I, the viceroy (the British ruler of India) asked Gandhi for help. Gandhi was to ask Indians to fight for Britain in the war. Many people were surprised that Gandhi agreed. But Gandhi still believed that if the Indian people wanted the rights of citizens of the British Empire, then they had to take on the duties as well. So, because Gandhi asked, Indian soldiers fought beside British soldiers in the war.

During the war, Britain half-promised India that it would soon rule itself. The promise was not kept. Unfair laws used during the war to control people for "security" reasons went on after the war. Trial without jury and imprisonment without trial continued. India's people felt cheated. It was clear that Britain did not mean to give up India.

The first struggle

For the first time, Gandhi decided to go against India's British government. As a

"In my humble opinion, noncooperation with evil is as much a duty as is cooperation with good."

Gandhi, speaking at his trial

protest, he decided on a *hartal,* a kind of general strike. He chose a day and declared that no one was to do business on that day. Shops must stay closed. Workers must strike. This began a twenty-eight-year struggle that was to end British rule.

Gandhi's hartals gained support. But they turned into riots in Delhi, Ahmedabad, Lahore, and Amritsar.

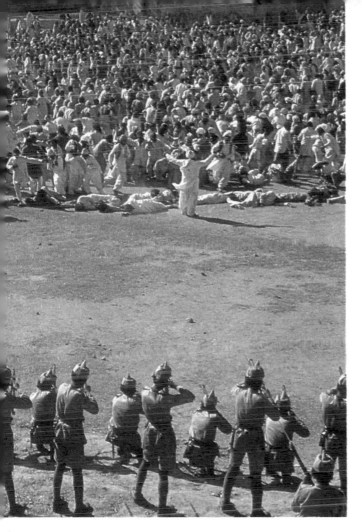

At the Sikhs' holy city of Amritsar, crowds gathered to show their support for Gandhi's nonviolent hurtal. It was held during a religious festival, and the men, women, and children were in a holiday mood. With no warning, soldiers opened fire. Hundreds were killed. This was the turning point for Gandhi. From then on, he directly opposed the British. (A scene from the film Gandhi.)

Gandhi saw that people had to be trained to behave well before civil disobedience would work. He fasted for seventy-two hours because of the riots and asked others to fast for twenty-four hours.

The Amritsar Massacre
On April 13, 1919, a meeting was held at Amritsar, in a large open space with high walls on three sides. The local British

army commander, General Reginald Dyer, decided to stop the meeting. Without warning, he ordered a small force of Indian soldiers to fire into the crowd. There was no escape. The soldiers fired for ten minutes, killing 379 people and wounding more than 7,200.

Dyer refused to let Indian medical workers help the wounded. He said later, "I thought I would be doing a jolly lot of good." He added, "Yes, I think it quite possible that I could have dispersed them without firing, but I was going to punish them."

When a British woman was hurt at Amritsar, Dyer issued the "Crawling Order." He posted armed soldiers along the street where the woman lived. The soldiers forced all Indians to crawl along her street on their bellies.

In 1920, Gandhi returned the British war medals he had received for his service in South Africa. He then wrote to the British viceroy: "I can retain neither respect nor affection for a government which has been moving from wrong to wrong in order to defend its immorality."

Many British people were ashamed of General Dyer's actions. His cruelty only made the Indians struggle harder against the British. Gandhi said, "I had faith in them until 1919, but the Amritsar Massacre changed my heart." He now believed that British rule had to be overthrown. He saw that self-rule and justice were not enough. The British must leave India.

The Indian National Congress

Gandhi joined a political group called the Indian National Congress. With his help, it became a huge organization with branches all over the country.

In December 1920, Gandhi asked the congress at Nagpur to call for *swaraj*, or self-rule. If possible, India would still belong to the British Empire but would leave the empire if it had to. The congress agreed. But Muslim leaders wanted to stay in the empire, so Hindu and Muslim leaders began to drift apart.

The group asked that Untouchables be treated well, and that villages start their own industries again. Gandhi hated the way that caste Hindus treated the Untouchables. He saw it as an insult and a threat to the Hindu religion. He wanted all Hindus to be equal and united. He also worked for basic

Gandhi urged Indians not to use British cloth. He encouraged them to spin their own yarn and make their own cloth. Every day, Gandhi spun two hundred yards of yarn.

Gandhi gave up the 1921 civil disobedience campaign after a group of his followers killed twenty-two policemen in Chauri Chaura. This is how the event was shown in the film Gandhi.

education for all. Finally, to promote national unity, he wanted Hindi, not English, used as the national language.

Spinning for victory

Gandhi saw the spinning wheel and home weaving as one way for villages to earn money and end poverty. He believed the terrible poverty of Indian villages was the result of towns and British textile mills taking work away from village craft industries.

The spinning wheel became a symbol of freedom from British rule. Ordinary people could afford one. It made use of hands that had nothing else to do. Its gentle hum was often heard at meetings of the Indian National Congress.

For the rest of his life, Gandhi spun two hundred yards of yarn each day. Even when he was at international meetings, working until 2:00 A.M., he did not sleep until he had done his spinning.

In 1921, Gandhi traveled all over India telling people that noncooperation — not helping the British — would bring India freedom. He asked people to stop buying British cloth and wearing foreign clothes. People listened to him. They threw their foreign-made clothes into fires. They stood outside shops that sold British cloth telling people not to buy. But they also burned merchants' stocks of foreign clothes. Burning warehouses lit the night sky. Gandhi was against actions such as this.

In October 1921, the congress called on soldiers and civil servants to leave their jobs. Lawyers stopped working. Schools and colleges were disrupted. Villagers refused to pay taxes. By December, twenty thousand people were in prison.

The British puzzled over the methods of the Indian leaders, especially gentle Gandhi. Dressed in a loincloth, the middle-aged, smiling Gandhi attracted thousands of people wherever he went. People walked for days just to see him.

"I came reluctantly to the conclusion that the British connection had made India more helpless than she was before, politically and economically. India has become so poor that she has little power of even resisting famines. . . . Before the British . . . India spun and wove in her millions of cottages just the supplement she needed for adding to her meager agricultural resources."

Mahatma Gandhi

33

As things came to a boil, riots spread throughout India. Gandhi fasted to show his sadness at the violence. Then, in February 1922, an angry crowd killed twenty-two policemen during "mass disobedience." Gandhi was sickened by this. At once, he stopped the protest against the British.

"It is better," said Gandhi, "to be charged with cowardice and weakness than . . . to sin against God. It is a million times better to appear untrue before the world than to be untrue to ourselves."

Many were disappointed. They felt let down. But Gandhi would not give up his method of nonviolence.

But the congress had shown its power. Hundreds of thousands of people were ready to work for freedom. They were willing to give up their jobs and to risk being put in prison. Gandhi was even more sure that people must be well trained to behave properly if nonviolence was to succeed. He fasted for five days because of the deaths.

The British government saw it could not ignore the Indian National Congress and India's demand for freedom.

Arrest and imprisonment

After the policemen were killed, Gandhi was arrested for rebellion against the government. At his trial, Gandhi pleaded guilty. "I hold it to be a virtue to [dislike] a government which . . . has done more harm to India than any previous system," he said.

"I am here therefore to invite and submit to the highest penalty that can be [given] for what in law is a deliberate crime and what appears to me to be the highest duty of a citizen."

Gandhi received the maximum sentence of six years and went cheerfully to prison again. "We must widen the prison gates," he said. "Freedom is to be wooed only inside prison walls." Gandhi spent his time in his cell, happily reading his books, spinning, and praying. He was let out of prison in 1924 because he was not well.

When he came out of prison, he found the Indian National Congress in a mess. The noncooperation movement had broken down. There was bad feeling between Muslims and Hindus. Gandhi spent the next few years trying to bring Hindus and Muslims closer together.

In these quiet years, Gandhi told people to use the spinning wheel and the hand loom. He said the wheel was like a restful prayer. He urged people to wear *khadi*, or homespun cloth. By buying khadi, the townspeople would help the peasants. Homespun cloth would bring together town and country, rich and poor. It became a sign that all who wore it were working for India's freedom.

"Yes, but we have something more important than guns. We have truth and justice — and time — on our side. You cannot hold down much longer 350 million people who are determined to be free. You will see!"
Mohandas K. Gandhi

Civil disobedience

In 1929, Gandhi, now sixty, began a new campaign of civil disobedience. It was to be different from the earlier protest. That one had tried to bring the government to a stop through strikes. The new campaign began with a protest against taxes. Gandhi asked people not to pay taxes, particularly the salt tax.

The highlight of the campaign was Gandhi's famous Salt March. The Salt March was a carefully planned and controlled twenty-four-day, two-

hundred-mile march. Now over sixty and looking frail, Gandhi led seventy-eight followers from his Sabarmati Ashram to the sea. By the time they reached the sea, several thousand people had joined them. At the sea, Gandhi bent down and picked up a handful of salt. The British treated it as a joke. What could picking up a handful of salt mean? They did not see how powerful and clever Gandhi was.

The Salt Tax was a symbol of the British government's power to tax.

Gandhi waited years before he began another civil disobedience campaign. He knew a nonviolent campaign could be dangerous if the people were not well behaved. In the Salt March, he and a band of followers walked very slowly to the sea — to pick up a handful of salt. (A scene from the film Gandhi.)

Above: Gandhi on the
Salt March with
Sarojini Naidu, a poet.
Gandhi was soon
arrested, and Naidu led
2,500 people in the
famous Dharasana Salt
Works protest.

Right: Gandhi bent
down to pick up a
handful of salt. This
was the signal for civil
disobedience all over
India. Hundreds of
thousands of Indians
broke the law by making
their own salt.

Therefore, it was a symbol of its power to rule. No one can live without salt, particularly in a hot country. The poorest peasant paid as much as the richest businessman. Many felt that it was very bad to tax something that nature provided free.

Gandhi said that Indians must ignore the Salt Tax and make their own salt. All over India, people began taking salt from the sea. At least sixty thousand people were arrested, including many leaders of the Indian National Congress. On the night of May 5, Gandhi was arrested. He was sleeping under a mango tree near the seashore. There was no trial — he was just locked away. Gandhi had hoped to be arrested; it was part of the plan.

Satyagraha in action

People went on protesting after Gandhi was in prison. Sarojini Naidu, a poet, led 2,500 congress members to the Dharasana Salt Works. It was defended by policemen with long steel-tipped sticks, called *lathi*. The protesters prayed, then marched forward. The first column was led by one of Gandhi's sons, Manilal. They were beaten very badly about their heads by the police. But they obeyed the rules of nonviolence and did not fight back. They fell where they stood. As the wounded fell with broken skulls, women dragged them away. A second column

"As we saw the abounding enthusiasm of the people and the way salt-making was spreading like a prairie fire, we felt a little . . . ashamed for having questioned . . . this method when it was first proposed by Gandhi. And we marveled at the amazing knack of the man to impress the multitude and make it act in an organized way."

Jawaharlal Nehru, leader of the Indian National Congress and later India's first prime minister

moved forward in silence. A British officer barked an order, and the police beat the protesters down. As they were dragged away, a new column formed.

American journalist Webb Miller witnessed this scene: "They marched steadily, with heads up, without . . . any possibility that they might escape serious injury or death. The police . . . beat down the column. There was no fight, no struggle; the marchers simply walked forward till struck down." Hundreds of newspapers published Miller's report. It made many people in Britain and the rest of the world think about what was happening in India.

The more unjust the British were, the more they played into Gandhi's hands. Within a year, Gandhi was called for talks with the British government's viceroy, Lord Irwin. Lord Irwin and Gandhi trusted each other. From their talks came the Irwin-Gandhi Pact. The agreement, among other things, allowed salt to be made free. Gandhi stopped the civil disobedience, and the British let all the prisoners go.

The Round Table Conference

In August 1931, Gandhi sailed to Britain. There, he attended a conference between British and Indian leaders to determine India's future. At the conference, Gandhi represented the Indian National

Opposite: The Dharasana Salt Works protest, as shown in the film Gandhi. It shows the 2,500 Gandhi followers, dressed in white, gathered in groups. Each group faced the four hundred Indian policemen who carried five-foot lathi with steel tips.

"Europe . . . is no longer regarded as the champion throughout the world of fair dealing . . . but as the upholder of western race supremacy and the exploiter of those outside her own borders."
Rabindranath Tagore, Indian writer who first called Gandhi the "Mahatma [Great Soul] in peasant's garb"

"All hope of reconciling India with the British Empire is lost. . . . I cannot understand how any government that calls itself civilized could deal as savagely and brutally with nonviolent, unresisting men as the British have this morning."
V. J. Patel, leader of the swaraj (self-rule) movement, at the time of Gandhi's arrest

Congress. Gandhi did not expect to achieve much at the conference. He was not interested in details of how a new government should work. But while in London, he won the hearts of many people and persuaded them that the Indians' demands were fair.

The British people were fascinated with Gandhi. Even newspaper reporters loved him. They asked him if in his loincloth he felt dressed enough for his visit to the king. Gandhi answered, "The king had enough on for both of us."

When he visited the cotton towns of Lancashire to explain why Indians were not buying British cloth, the workers cheered Gandhi. Many of them had lost jobs because Indians stopped buying British cloth. But they liked the fact that he took the trouble to come and talk with them. Their own leaders hardly ever did.

The conference was a failure. It actually widened differences between the Indian groups. Gandhi said, "They went into the conference Muslims and Sikhs and Untouchables, and they came out of it Muslims and Sikhs and Untouchables — and never at any moment was the Indian nation there." He left for India.

The "Children of God"

Within three weeks of his return to India, Gandhi was back in prison. He began to

Gandhi arriving at 10 Downing Street, London, the home of the British prime minister. The British leaders were surprised at how well he spoke and that he never tired. He always smiled, and talked both to the public and to the newspapers. He kept five secretaries busy and got only four hours of sleep a night.

work for the Untouchables and began a fast to the death. It made many Indians think about how they treated the Untouchables. Soon, there were some improvements in the way they were elected to the congress and the way people behaved toward them. For instance, they were allowed to use wells and temples that had been closed to them. Other Hindus welcomed them.

After he came out of prison in 1933, Gandhi began a twelve-thousand-mile Harijan tour to collect money for the Untouchables. His fight for them was only partially successful. The fight goes

Hundreds of thousands of Lancashire cotton workers were unemployed because people in India, led by Gandhi, were refusing to buy British cloth. Yet Gandhi was welcomed by the unemployed people. He told them of the terrible poverty in India. The workers felt that Gandhi understood their problems.

A village of Untouchables in Maharashtra, in western India. Gandhi thought the caste system — especially the treatment of Untouchables — was a very bad side of Hinduism. He called the Untouchables the Harijans, or "Children of God."

on still. Today, government officials and community leaders test laws by taking Untouchables into barbershops and tea shops where they are still not allowed.

In these quieter years, Gandhi worked hard to bring the Hindus and the Muslims closer together. He was heartbroken to see that the two groups were drifting farther apart. He was afraid that India's independence would divide the two completely. He said that freedom from Britain should be delayed if it meant avoiding that division.

Storm clouds of war

When World War II began in 1939, India was not ready for it. On the whole, leaders of the Indian National Congress supported Britain in the fight. But they resigned when the viceroy decided — without asking the people — that India was also at war. To win support from the congress, the British promised India freedom after the war.

Gandhi asked for India's freedom at once. Still, he was on the side of Britain and its allies. He did not want to seize independence violently. "We do not seek our independence out of Britain's ruin," he said.

In August 1942, Gandhi made a speech asking the British to leave India. Perhaps he did not understand what his words would do. Certainly he was sorry for the terrible riots that followed his "Quit India" speech.

Kasturba's death

Two days after his "Quit India" speech, Gandhi was put in prison again. Violence broke out all over India.

It was a time of great sadness for Gandhi. His secretary, Mahadev Desai, died suddenly. Then his wife became sick. Gandhi and Kasturba spent the last months of their lives together in prison. They had been married since they were children. Gandhi was holding her when

"To see the . . . spirit of truth face to face, one must be able to love the meanest of creatures as oneself."

Gandhi, in his autobiography

"I hold myself to be incapable of hating any being on earth. By a long course of prayerful discipline, I have ceased for over forty years to hate anybody. I know this is a big claim. Nevertheless, I make it in all humility."

Mohandas K. Gandhi

she died. Shortly after Kasturba's death, Gandhi was let out of prison. He was very sick. The viceroy was afraid there would be more violence if he died while in prison.

The transfer of power

In 1945, after the end of World War II, the new government in Britain promised to give India freedom. Other leaders of the Indian National Congress were allowed out of prison. There were elections. The congress was still the largest political group, but it was no longer supported by the Muslims.

During the war, the Muslim League, led by Mohammed Ali Jinnah, had gained support for a Muslim state of Pakistan. This idea, known as Partition, would divide India into two separate countries — one country for Hindus and the other for Muslims. Gandhi and the congress hated this idea.

The British government made one last attempt to keep India a single state. It failed when talks between the Indian National Congress and the Muslim League broke down.

The viceroy, Lord Archibald Wavell, invited Gandhi's follower, Jawaharlal Nehru, to form a temporary government. Nehru asked Mohammed Ali Jinnah for help in running the government. Nehru even offered members of the Muslim

League several government posts. But Jinnah would not agree.

In August, the Muslim League decided to have a "Direct Action Day" to force Britain to let them have a separate Muslim state. Terrible fighting broke out around Calcutta. Four thousand people were killed. Another fifteen thousand people were injured in shootings, stabbings, and burnings. The violence spread to East Bengal. Muslim gangs roamed about, forcing Hindus to become Muslims or die.

The news horrified Gandhi. He decided to go to East Bengal himself. He said, "I intend to bury myself in East Bengal until such a time as the Hindus and Muslims learn to live together in peace. . . . I do not know what I shall be able to do there. All I know is that I won't be at peace unless I go."

Gandhi found this the most difficult task of his life. He was now seventy-seven years old and very weak. He walked barefoot from village to village, trying to calm people. He held prayer meetings. He called for courage, truth, and forgiveness.

From East Bengal, Gandhi went to Bihar. There the riot victims were Muslims, not Hindus. Again, Gandhi held prayer meetings. He tried to get Muslims back in their homes and collected money from Hindus to help

A riot in Bombay shows Hindu-Muslim violence. Over half a million people were killed while India was being freed from British rule. Many people believe that millions more would have died if Gandhi had not tried to make peace.

Muslims. He said he would not leave until there was peace. A month later, the killing stopped.

The last viceroy

Jinnah was still demanding India's partition. Britain's prime minister, Clement R. Attlee, gave up trying to make the Muslim League and the Indian National Congress agree. He decided that Britain would hand over power to the Indians by June 1948.

The new and last viceroy of India, Lord Louis Mountbatten, arrived in Delhi in March 1947. He came to the job youthful and fresh, with a knowledge of India's problems. The prime minister had given him full power to do what he thought best for India. Almost at once, he sent a message to Gandhi that he wished to see him. Of their first meeting, Mountbatten later said: "Certainly I was quite unprepared to meet such a lovable old man, with a warm, human manner, great good humour, charming manners, and perhaps most unexpectedly of all, an unfailing sense of humour."

But time was short. Mountbatten said, "I could sense a real tragedy round the corner if we did not act very fast — civil war in its worst form. Beside that, Partition, much as many of us hated it, seemed a much lesser evil."

Gandhi went to East Bengal when he heard that people were being killed. Gandhi said he would die to stop the killing between Hindus and Muslims. He tramped from village to village, calming the people.

49

Lord Louis and Lady Edwina Mountbatten invited Gandhi to tea. Mountbatten believed that only Gandhi could help India become free from three hundred years of British rule peacefully. He came to see Gandhi as the greatest person he'd ever met. He said of Gandhi, "His life was one of truth, toleration, and love. . . . India, indeed the world, will not see the likes of him again, perhaps for centuries."

Mountbatten's team worked around the clock. In six weeks, they produced a plan for India's independence. But Jinnah was not happy with it. He insisted on Partition. But he wasn't satisfied with what he called his "moth-eaten Pakistan."

The main argument was over two main provinces in northern India, Bengal and Punjab. Both of these provinces had large Muslim populations. Jinnah insisted on Partition so that Muslims would not be outnumbered by the Hindus in India. Mountbatten and the Indian National Congress said that the two provinces Jinnah wanted must also be partitioned. Both provinces had large non-Muslim religious groups. These

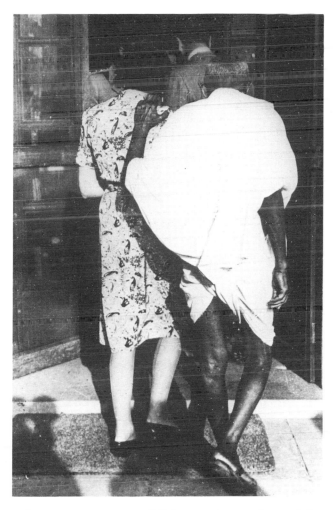

Gandhi and Lady Mountbatten enter the viceroy's house for the discussions on India's independence. It was a sad time for Gandhi as he tried to stop India from being broken up into separate Hindu and Muslim countries.

other groups would be outnumbered by Muslims. So they must be separated.

In the end, Pakistan became a country of two parts. One part — West Pakistan — was formed in northwestern India. The other — East Bengal — was formed in northeastern India. The two were separated by one thousand miles of Indian land. The eastern part of Pakistan, East Bengal, broke away from

August 15, 1947: Independence Day at the Red Fort in Delhi. Gandhi had spent forty years of his life working for and waiting for this day. But he did not go to the ceremony. He was still in Calcutta trying to make peace between the Hindu and Muslim groups.

the country in early 1971. It became an independent country called Bangladesh.

Partition

For many of India's people, August 15, 1947, was one of history's greatest days. One-fifth of the world's people gained independence that day. There was great rejoicing. But Gandhi did not celebrate.

"My independence," he said, "has not yet come. There is no reason for festivals and merriments like this."

People had rejected Gandhi's ideal of unity. He had struggled toward this goal all his life. Now he felt let down by his friends and fellow citizens.

Gandhi had always said he would like to live to be 125 years old. As the violence began again, he said at his prayer meetings, "I wanted to be 125. Now I have lost interest in life." But even in these last months of his life, Gandhi still had more battles to fight.

"The old man has done it again"

In August 1947, Gandhi was in Calcutta. The city had already had a year of terrible violence. A well-known Indian writer, Sudhin Datta, remembered later, "For a year it had seemed as if it was not worth living in Calcutta. And then Gandhi had come. The first day I think they threw

Twelve million people fled in opposite directions as Muslims left India for the newly created country of Pakistan and Hindus fled out of Pakistan to India. (See map on page 62.) This picture, showing people leaving their homes, is from the film Gandhi.

brickbats at him, and sticks at him, and then of course he talked to them, and slowly in two or three days' time the atmosphere changed and on the fourteenth what we saw is perhaps the only miracle I have seen in my life."

The miracle was that Muslims and Hindus were dancing and celebrating together. Soldiers pinned little flags on their bayonets. Everywhere, people said, "The old man has done it again!"

Still, Gandhi could not celebrate. By the end of the month, violence began again. Gandhi told the people he would fast to the death. Only peace would end this fast. Within four days, Calcutta's

The British viceroy, Lord Mountbatten, called Gandhi his "one-man boundary force." Thousands of troops could not stop the violence in East Bengal, but Gandhi did. He walked through mud and swamps to talk about his methods of nonviolence. And everywhere he went, he brought peace.

citizens brought him written promises of peace. Gandhi broke his fast.

A one-man boundary force

Gandhi went to the Punjab, where 55,000 soldiers were stationed to stop violence. As Mountbatten later said, "When the trouble started, the 55,000-man boundary force in the Punjab was swamped by riots, but my one-man boundary force brought peace in Bengal."

In September, Gandhi began his last journey — back to Delhi. Refugees were fleeing the city as others poured in. All over northern India, people were leaving their homes. No one really knows how many lives were lost in these weeks of violence, but a figure of two hundred thousand killed may be low. Over fifteen million people fled from India to Pakistan or from Pakistan to India.

Gandhi went to the refugee camps. Some housed Sikhs and Hindus driven from the Punjab. Some housed Muslims chased from their homes in Delhi. He held daily prayer meetings in the garden of Birla House, where he was staying. He read from the Hindu Bhagavad Gita, the Muslim Koran, and the Jewish-Christian Bible. Hundreds of people came to hear.

The last fast

In January 1948, Gandhi announced that he was going to begin a fast. "The fast

Three dead bodies lie in the streets of Calcutta. About three thousand people — mainly Muslims — had died during the previous five days. Calcutta was the scene of the most violent fighting before and during independence. Only Gandhi was able to calm the city — and then only by another fast. He nearly died, but he did get the peace he wanted.

Gandhi with his two great-nieces, Manu and Abhu. He called them his "walking sticks." This picture was taken the day before Gandhi was killed. He was hardly able to walk because he was so weak from his fast that had brought peace to Delhi.

will end," he said, "when I am satisfied that there is a reunion of hearts of all communities." He was seventy-eight. It was his eighteenth great fast. It was also to be the final fast of his life.

By the third day, he had persuaded the Indian government to make a large payment of money due to Pakistan. Many Hindus were very angry. They thought Gandhi was fasting to help the Muslims who were at war with India in the province of Kashmir. Crowds of Sikhs and Hindus gathered outside Birla House. They chanted "Blood for blood!" and "Let Gandhi die!"

On the sixth day, the leaders of the different communities in Delhi brought promises to Gandhi. They promised they would make every effort to restore peace and friendship, even at the cost of their own lives. Gandhi was pleased with their vows. He broke his fast.

He went straight back to work. He worked furiously on plans that would give power to the people and put life back into the villages. In the evening, he always held a prayer meeting. At one, someone threw a bomb, but no one was hurt. The Indian minister of home affairs was afraid Gandhi would be killed. Gandhi said, "If I have to die, I should like to die at a prayer meeting. You are wrong in believing that you can protect me from harm. God is my protector."

The death of Gandhi

On the last day of his life, Gandhi got up in the clear Delhi dawn at 3:00 A.M. He worked, held meetings, and spent time in prayer. That evening, he hurried out of Birla House because he was late for prayers. Robert Stimson, a British reporter who was there, reported that "his arms were resting lightly on the shoulders of two companions, and he was smiling. There were only two or three hundred people in the garden, and they pressed eagerly towards him. . . . As he . . . approached the crowd . . . he raised his hands in [a greeting]. He was still smiling. A thick-set man . . . was in the

Each evening in Delhi, Gandhi would leave his rooms in Birla House to say evening prayers in the garden. On January 30, 1948, he was killed on his way to the waiting crowd. This photograph is from the film Gandhi.

सच पर विश्वास रखो
सच ही सोचो सच ही करो
BELIEVE IN TRUTH
THINK TRUT. &
LIVE T UTH

A statue of Mahatma Gandhi in Delhi. In towns and villages throughout India, there are statues in memory of Gandhi. The words on it appear in both Hindi and English. They say, "Believe in truth, think truth, and live truth."

front of the crowd. He moved a step towards Mr. Gandhi, took out a revolver, and fired several shots."

Gandhi murmured "Hey Rama" ("Oh God"), stood a moment as blood oozed into his clothes, and then fell dead.

Lord Mountbatten told the author some years ago, "I went round at once to Birla House. There was a large crowd around the house already . . . everyone in tears. Gandhi looked very peaceful in death, but I dreaded what his death might bring.

"Someone in the crowd shouted out, 'It was a Muslim who did it!' I turned immediately and said: 'You fool, don't you know it was a Hindu?' Of course I didn't know — no one knew at that stage. But I did know this, if it was a Muslim, we were lost. There would be civil war without fail."

The man turned out to be Nathuram Godse, a Hindu. He was later hanged. Gandhi's funeral took place on the banks of the holy river Jumna. A million people waited for the procession. Gandhi's ashes were scattered in the sacred rivers of India and in the sea at Bombay.

Prime Minister Nehru gave the news of Gandhi's death to the Indian people over the radio: "The light has gone out of our lives, and there is darkness everywhere, and I do not know what to tell you and how to say it. Our beloved leader, Bapu as we call him, the father of our nation, is now no more."

Gandhi's few belongings show that he did not believe in owning things. These were some of the things he used at the time of his death: chappals (wooden sandals), a cheap nickel-plated watch, spectacles, a bowl, a spoon, and a book of songs.

Gandhi's gifts

Later, Nehru said, "'The light has gone out,' I said, and yet I was wrong. For the light that shone in this country was no ordinary light. The light that has [lit up] this country for this many years will

"Between the two world wars, force reigned supreme. . . . it was natural for the weaker to lie down before the stronger. Then came Gandhi, chasing out of his country, almost singlehandedly, the greatest military power on earth. He taught the world that there are higher things than force, higher even than life itself."
Albert Szent-Györgyi, Nobel laureate

"Gandhi was inevitable. If humanity is to progress, Gandhi is inescapable. He lived, thought and acted, inspired by a vision of humanity evolving toward a world of peace and harmony. We may ignore him at our own risk."
Martin Luther King, Jr.

[light up] this country for many more years, and a thousand years later, that light will be seen in this country, and the world will see it. . . . For that light represented the living truth, and the eternal man was with us with his eternal truth reminding us of the right path, drawing us from error, taking this ancient country to freedom."

The poor man's friend

Gandhi taught the Hindus to be proud of their own culture and traditions. By his own courage, he taught people to stand up for themselves. He was loved by peasants and factory workers because he fought for them. He won the affection of Muslims because of his work for them.

Gandhi, wearing only his loincloth, had once visited King George V of Britain at Buckingham Palace. The king asked, "Mr. Gandhi, how is India doing?" Gandhi pointed to his skinny limbs and his poor loincloth. "Look at me," he said. "You will know from me what India is like."

Perhaps this was the secret of Gandhi's appeal. Many Indians saw him as a symbol of India. Humble and poor, he showed what their lives were like. He could talk with them. He expressed their thoughts. He was one of them.

To find out more . . .

Organizations

The groups listed below work to make life better for the people
that Gandhi struggled to set free. If you would like to know more
about their work or would like to offer your help, write to them at
the addresses listed below. When you write, be sure to tell them
exactly what you would like to know. Also include your name,
address, and age.

American Friends Service
   Committee
1501 Cherry Street
Philadelphia, PA 19102

Save the Children
Public Affairs Office
54 Wilton Road
Westport, CT 06880

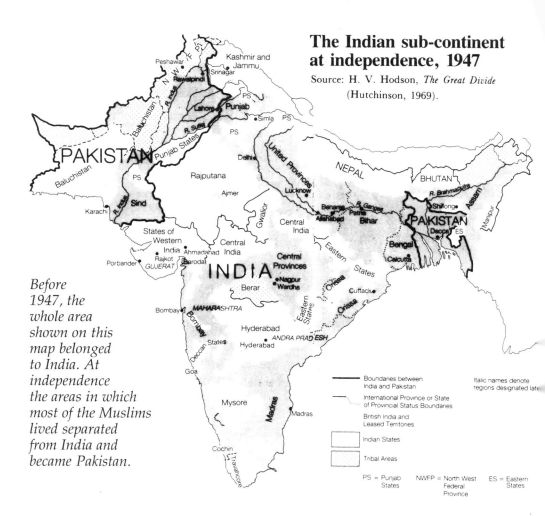

The Indian sub-continent at independence, 1947

Source: H. V. Hodson, *The Great Divide* (Hutchinson, 1969).

Before 1947, the whole area shown on this map belonged to India. At independence the areas in which most of the Muslims lived separated from India and became Pakistan.

Boundaries between India and Pakistan

International Province or State of Provincial Status Boundaries

British India and Leased Territories

Indian States

Tribal Areas

PS = Punjab States

NWFP = North West Federal Province

ES = Eastern States

Italic names denote regions designated late

CARE
660 First Avenue
New York, NY 10016

Oxfam America
115 Broadway
Boston, MA 02116

Lutheran World Relief
390 Park Avenue South
New York, NY 10016

United Nations Children's Fund
331 East 38th Street
New York, NY 10016

Missionaries of Charity
335 East 145th Street
New York, NY 10451

World Vision
919 West Huntington Drive
Monrovia, CA 91016

Books

The following books will tell you more about Mahatma Gandhi, India, and events in India's history. If you would like to learn more about these subjects, check your local library or bookstore to see if they have these books or if someone will order them for you.

About Mahatma Gandhi —
Gandhi. Hunter (Franklin Watts)
Gandhi. Spink (David & Charles)
Mahatma Gandhi. Faber and Faber (Julian Messner)

About India —
India. Caldwell (Chelsea House)
India: An Ancient Land, A New Nation. Sarin (Dillon)

List of new words

ahimsa
> A Hindi word for nonviolence to all living creatures.

ashram
> A religious community made up of people who lead a simple life and grow their own food.

Boer War
> The war fought in South Africa from 1899 to 1902 between the Boers (now called Afrikaners) and the British.

caste system
> A strict system of social groups in Hindu society. There are four main groups: Brahmin, Kshatriya, Vaisya, and Sudra. There is also a large group of "Untouchables" who are outcasts, people of such low standing that they are outside the system altogether.

civil disobedience
> A nonviolent way of protesting against a law one dislikes.

People who are practicing civil disobedience may refuse to pay taxes or may hold sit-ins or may march through the streets. Civil disobedience differs from traditional lawbreaking in that protesters do not harm others and sometimes do not even defend themselves. Also, the protesters often expect to be arrested as a result of their actions and accept that as part of the risk. This is the way of satyagraha which Gandhi taught.

Congress, Indian National
This group was founded to try to get Indians a place in the government of India. It became the main party to work for independence. It once had many Muslim members, but is now mainly Hindu. Since independence came in 1947, it has ruled India for all but three years.

dhoti
Hindi for "loincloth"; a cloth that men in some cultures wrap about themselves and wear as Westerners would wear pants.

durbar
Hindi for "ruler's court"; formerly, an official ceremony that was held by a native prince or by a British ruler or governor in India or Africa.

Harijan
"Child of God" in Hindi; Gandhi's name for the Untouchables.

hartal
A kind of national strike in India; shops and businesses close as a political protest but the day is spent in fasting and other religious practices.

Hindu
A follower of Hinduism, one of the five major religions of the world and the main religion of India. Fear of a religious war between Hindus and Muslims resulted in Partition in 1947.

khadi

A Hindi word for a kind of homespun cloth. To unify India, Gandhi urged Indians to wear khadi rather than British cloth.

Moguls

A Muslim dynasty of India that reigned from 1526 until the mid-eighteenth century. Its founder, Babur, was descended from Genghis Khan and Tamerlane (Timur the Lame).

Muslim

A follower of Islam, one of the five major religions of the world. Strife between Hindus and Muslims was the reason for Partition in 1947.

Pakistan

The two areas in northern India having more Muslims than Hindus, which became independent at Partition. In 1971, East Pakistan broke away and is now known as Bangladesh.

Partition

The separation of India in 1947 into India and Pakistan. India was mostly Hindu and Pakistan mostly Muslim. Over twelve million people left their homes for one country or the other because Muslims and Hindus were killing each other.

satyagraha

The force of "holding on to the truth." This was the Hindi name that Gandhi used for his nonviolent efforts to change unfair treatment of Indians by the British.

Untouchables

People who were considered below the caste system. They did such jobs as sweeping roads and cleaning bathrooms. Members of the top caste, Brahmins, believed that if even their shadow touched an Untouchable, they would become dirty and would have to bathe themselves.

viceroy

The governor of a country or province who rules in the name of a king or queen.

Important dates

1869   **October 2** — Mohandas Karamchand Gandhi is born in Porbandar.

1882   Gandhi marries Kasturba. Both are thirteen years old.

1888   **September** — Gandhi sails to England to study law.

1891   **June** — He returns to India after becoming a lawyer.

1893   **April** — Gandhi sails to South Africa.

1899-   In the Boer War, Gandhi supports Britain and
1902   organizes the Indian Ambulance Corps.

1907   The first satyagraha campaign begins in South Africa. Gandhi is sent to prison four times in the next five years.

1914   **June** — South Africa changes some laws unfair to Indians.

1915   **January** — Gandhi returns to India and starts an ashram. Shortly thereafter, he begins working for self-rule through the Indian National Congress.

1919   **February** — The Rowlatt Act allows British courts to try Indians in secret and without juries; it also delays any consideration of independence for ten years. Gandhi calls a nationwide hartal in protest.
April 13 — The massacre at Amritsar takes place.

1922   **March** — Gandhi is sentenced to six years in jail.

1924   **February** — Gandhi leaves jail early because of ill health.

1928   The Indian National Congress calls for independence.

1930   **January 1** — Jawaharlal Nehru calls for Britain to fulfill the promises of the Rowlatt Act.
March 12-April 16 — Gandhi leads the Salt March to Dandi
May — Gandhi is arrested with other Indian leaders just before the demonstration at the Dharasana Salt Works.

1931   **January** — Gandhi is released from jail and negotiates the Irwin-Gandhi Pact with the current viceroy.
May — Gandhi meets with King George V in London.

1932   **January** — Just days after his return from England, Gandhi is arrested again; he is released in May 1933.
September — Gandhi starts a fast to the death to protest the treatment of the Untouchables.

1939   World War II breaks out; anti-British activities are now considered treasonous.

1942   The Indian National Congress holds its "Quit India" vote. Gandhi and other leaders are arrested. Violent riots follow.

1944   **February 22** — Kasturba dies in prison.
May 6 — Gandhi is released.

1946   **April** — Jinnah calls for a separate Pakistan.
August — Muslims massacre Hindus in Calcutta.

1947   **August 15** — Independence is declared.
September — Gandhi begins a fast to protest Hindu-Muslim violence.

1948   **January 30** — Gandhi is assassinated by Nathuram Godse.

Index